This

THOMAS & FRIENDS

Annual
belongs to

....

....

Contents

EGMONT
We bring stories to life

First published in Great Britain in 2010 by Egmont UK Limited,
239 Kensington High Street, London W8 6SA

Written by Pippa Shaw
Designed by Martin Aggett
All rights reserved.

Thomas the Tank Engine & Friends™

CREATED BY BRITT ALLCROFT
Based on the Railway Series by the Reverend W Awdry
© 2010 Gullane (Thomas) LLC. A HIT Entertainment company.
Thomas the Tank Engine & Friends and Thomas & Friends are trademarks of Gullane (Thomas) Limited.
Thomas the Tank Engine & Friends and Design is Reg. U.S. Pat. & Tm. Off.

ISBN 978 1 4052 5240 9
1 3 5 7 9 10 8 6 4 2
Printed in Italy

"Hello, everyone! My name is Thomas.
I live here on the Island of Sodor
with all my friends.
Let's go and meet some of them."

Thomas and His Friends

"**Hello!**
I'm Sir Topham Hatt, but everyone calls me **The Fat Controller**. Let's go on a tour of my railway and meet some of my **Really Useful Engines.**"

Thomas

Thomas is a **cheeky** little blue engine. He gets himself into all kinds of scrapes, but he always puts things right again.

James

Sometimes James can be a little vain; after all, he is the only **shiny** bright red engine on Sodor.

Gordon

Gordon is the **fastest** engine on Sodor and likes to boast about it!

Charlie

Charlie is a cheery chap. He loves to have **fun**, just like Thomas!

Emily

Emily is a very **bossy** engine who likes to show the other engines how things should be done.

Henry

Henry is a very **trusted** engine who huffs and puffs his way around Sodor.

Edward

Everybody likes Edward! He's **friendly** to all the engines on Sodor and has the number 2 on his side.

Harold

Harold the helicopter has **whirring** propellers that the engines can hear as he flies through the air.

Percy

Percy loves to pull the mail train. He'll do whatever it takes to be **Really Useful!**

Hiro

Hiro was the first engine on Sodor, and was once called the **Master of the Railway.**

Toby

Toby is a little tram who is always **happy** to work with his loyal coach, Henrietta!

Rosie

Rosie is a **jolly** purple engine. She loves working with Thomas!

Spencer

Spencer has the **shiniest** paint of all the engines on Sodor. He belongs to the Duke and Duchess of Boxford.

Around the Island

The **Island of Sodor** is a busy place indeed! Let's look at some of the places that the engines visit on The Fat Controller's Railway ...

GORDON'S HILL

This is the steepest hill on Sodor. It is called 'Gordon's Hill' because Gordon the Big Engine once got stuck pulling a goods train up it!

TIDMOUTH SHEDS

At the end of a busy day, Thomas and his friends puff back here to share stories of their adventures before going to sleep.

KNAPFORD STATION

Knapford Station is the biggest and busiest station on Sodor. The engines are always chuffing past each other and peeping a friendly "hello!" in this station.

Can you see Thomas? Is he puffing to Wellsworth or the Airport?

BRENDAM DOCKS

Brendam Docks is home to lots of engines and machines.

Cranky is a bad-tempered crane. He spends his days loading and unloading ships and engines here.

Peel Godred

Quarry

Kirk Machan

Arlesburgh

Ffarquhar

Quarry

Tidmouth

Knapford

Wellsworth

Maron

Suddery

Brendam

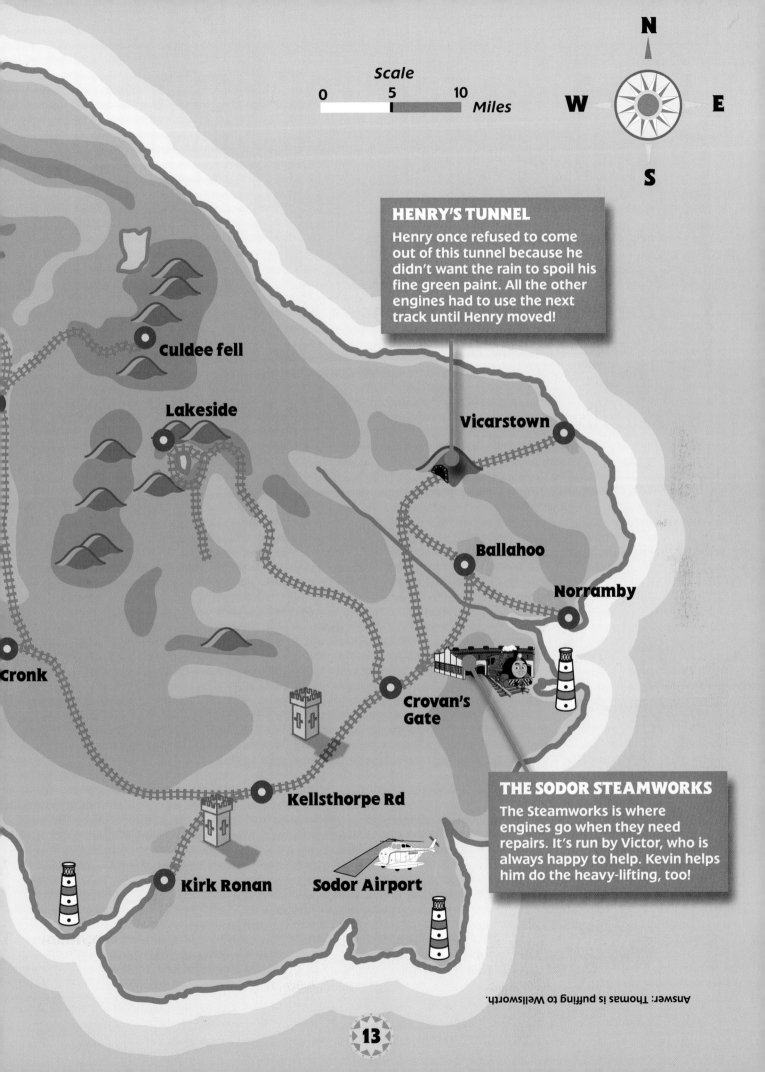

Scale

0   5   10 Miles

N W E S

Culdee fell

Lakeside

HENRY'S TUNNEL

Henry once refused to come out of this tunnel because he didn't want the rain to spoil his fine green paint. All the other engines had to use the next track until Henry moved!

Vicarstown

Ballahoo

Norramby

Cronk

Crovan's Gate

Kellsthorpe Rd

THE SODOR STEAMWORKS

The Steamworks is where engines go when they need repairs. It's run by Victor, who is always happy to help. Kevin helps him do the heavy-lifting, too!

Kirk Ronan

Sodor Airport

Answer: Thomas is puffing to Wellsworth.

★ The Fat Controller's Test ★

How much can you remember from meeting Thomas and his friends? Answer these questions by ticking the boxes to find out!

1 Who is the only bright red engine on the Island of Sodor?

a Percy ☐

b James ☐

c Henry ☐

2 Who has a loyal coach called Henrietta?

a Thomas ☐   **b** Edward ☐   **c** Toby ☐

3 Who has whirring propellers that make a noise?

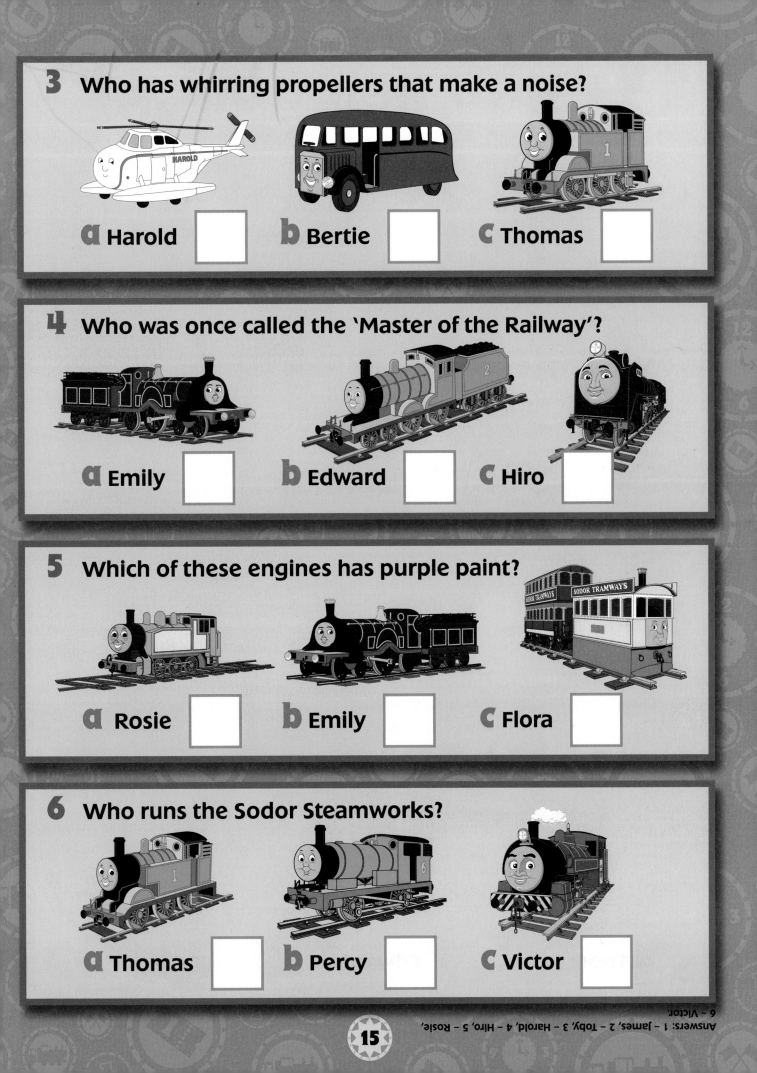

a Harold ☐　**b** Bertie ☐　**c** Thomas ☐

4 Who was once called the 'Master of the Railway'?

a Emily ☐　**b** Edward ☐　**c** Hiro ☐

5 Which of these engines has purple paint?

a Rosie ☐　**b** Emily ☐　**c** Flora ☐

6 Who runs the Sodor Steamworks?

a Thomas ☐　**b** Percy ☐　**c** Victor ☐

Hiro Helps Out

One day, Hiro puffed into Knapford Station and saw the oddest sight. The Fat Controller was rushing around, red-faced and without his top hat! Hiro was worried.

"Can I help you, Sir?" he asked The Fat Controller.

"I have a **very busy** day, Hiro," The Fat Controller told him.

"I have too much to do and not enough time!"

And with that, The Fat Controller hurried away.

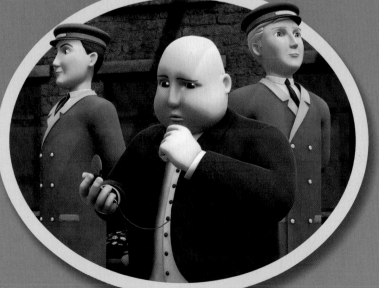

Just then, Edward puffed into the station looking for The Fat Controller. He had to pick up some visitors from Brendam Docks but he didn't know where to take them!

Hiro didn't want to bother The Fat Controller. He already had enough to do!

"Take them to the Hills, Edward," Hiro said, helpfully. "They'll like it there.'

So Edward puffed away to the Docks and Hiro **wheeshed** to the Water Tower.

On the way, Hiro saw Thomas. He was going to Knapford to see The Fat Controller about some benches and tables.

"Go and visit your friend, Farmer Trotter, instead," Hiro suggested. "The Fat Controller is **very busy** now."

So Thomas cheerfully chuffed away to the farm.

On Hiro chugged. As he steamed up to the next junction, he passed Percy pulling a flatbed of ducks.

"I have to find The Fat Controller," Percy said. "He will tell me where to take these ducks for a swim!"

But Hiro still didn't want to bother The Fat Controller.

"Perhaps you could puff to the pond at Fenland. The ducks will like it there," Hiro said.

Percy pumped his pistons and left for Fenland, leaving behind a very happy Hiro. He was the Master of the Railway again, just like in the old days!

Just then, The Fat Controller's car pulled up to the junction.

"Hiro!" he said. "I've heard some worrying news. Farmer McColl is waiting for his ducks, and we can't find the tables, chairs or the audience for the tea-time concert either!"

Hiro gasped. What a muddle he'd made! He was only trying to help!

"I'm sorry, Sir," Hiro said. "I knew you were busy, and I didn't want to bother you. So I told the engines what to do."

"Hiro, nothing is more important to me than my engines being **Really Useful**," The Fat Controller replied.

"I was wrong, but I will put this right," said Hiro, as he steamed away.

Hiro **clickety-clacked** along the track until he'd told Edward, Thomas and Percy to go to Knapford straight away. The Fat Controller gave them their orders and everyone puffed happily away.

All except Hiro – The Fat Controller had thought of a special way for Hiro to be Really Useful … Hiro was to help him in Knapford. Nothing could have made Hiro happier!

Two the Same

Hiro likes to be **helpful**. Find two pictures of him that look exactly the same. Circle the letters when you have found them.

a

b

c

d

e

Counting Fun

The engines are getting their jobs for the day! **How many engines** can you count at Tidmouth Sheds? Colour in the correct number below.

1 2 3 4 5 6 7

Names and Numbers

Some of the engines on Sodor have **numbers** as well as names! Colour in the right number for each engine.

1 2 3 4 5 6 7

Thomas

James

1 2 3 4 5 6 7

1 2 3 4 5 6 7

Percy

★ Creaky Cranky ★

It was an **exciting day** on Sodor. The Duke and Duchess of Boxford were holding a spring party. At Brendam Docks, Cranky the Crane was busy unloading everything for the party, when Thomas cheerfully chuffed on to the dockside. "It's the Duke and Duchess' party today!" smiled Thomas.

"I don't go to parties," grumbled Cranky. "I'm stuck here."

"You're creaky, Cranky! Is everything too heavy for you?" teased Thomas.

But Cranky wasn't in the mood for jokes.

"You couldn't pull anything heavy, Tiny Thomas! That's why Henry and James have the heavy loads today!" he snapped.

"I'm as **strong** as any other engine, and I'll prove it!" Thomas told the crane as he puffed off to find James. There was more than enough time to make his delivery later.

Thomas found James at the wash down.

"Shall I deliver your wood and barrels for you?" he asked. "Then you can get ready for the party."

James thought it was a wonderful idea, and soon Thomas was coupled to his heavy flatbed.

Huffing and puffing, Thomas set off for the Docks.

He **dared** Cranky to try to lift the flatbed. He was sure the creaky crane wouldn't be able to do it. But Cranky did! Thomas was very cross! He steamed off to find Henry.

Henry was waiting at the coal hopper, so Thomas offered to take his straw bales for him. Henry was delighted.

"Thank you, Thomas!" he smiled. Thomas huffed hard to get the flatbed back to the Docks, but Cranky managed to lift it up. Thomas was even crosser! Suddenly, an idea flew into his funnel. "Lift me, Cranky!" he told the big crane.

Cranky didn't want to let Thomas win, so he lowered his hook towards him. As soon as Thomas was safely attached, he started to lift the little engine up.

Then there was trouble! Cranky's crane arm stuttered and stopped! Thomas was stuck in the sky!

The Fat Controller arrived. "You are causing confusion and delay," he told Thomas. "Cranky is broken, and no deliveries have been made for the party."

Thomas was very sorry. He knew it was all his fault, and as soon as the Engineer lowered him back on to the tracks, he set about making things right. He asked strong Spencer to take the wood and straw to the party.

Then Thomas pumped his pistons to collect new parts for Cranky from Victor and Kevin at the Steamworks.

Thomas rushed back to the Docks. Cranky could see that the new parts were heavy, and he was very grateful.

"Thank you, Thomas," he said. "You're not so 'Tiny', after all."

"And you're not 'creaky' either," said Thomas. The two friends smiled at each other. Thomas decided not to go back to the party, after all. He and Cranky had their **own party** instead!

Spot the Difference ★

Thomas and his friend Charlie are chuffing across Sodor being Really Useful.

1

These two pictures look the same, but 6 things are different in picture 2.

Colour in a steam cloud for each one you find.

Engine Parts

Thomas needs all of his parts to work perfectly to be **Really Useful**. Draw lines to match the words to Thomas' body.

Driver's cab

funnel

whistle

wheels

buffers

coupling hook

Which Piece?

Thomas is at the Steamworks, ready for action!

Which of the pieces below completes the picture?

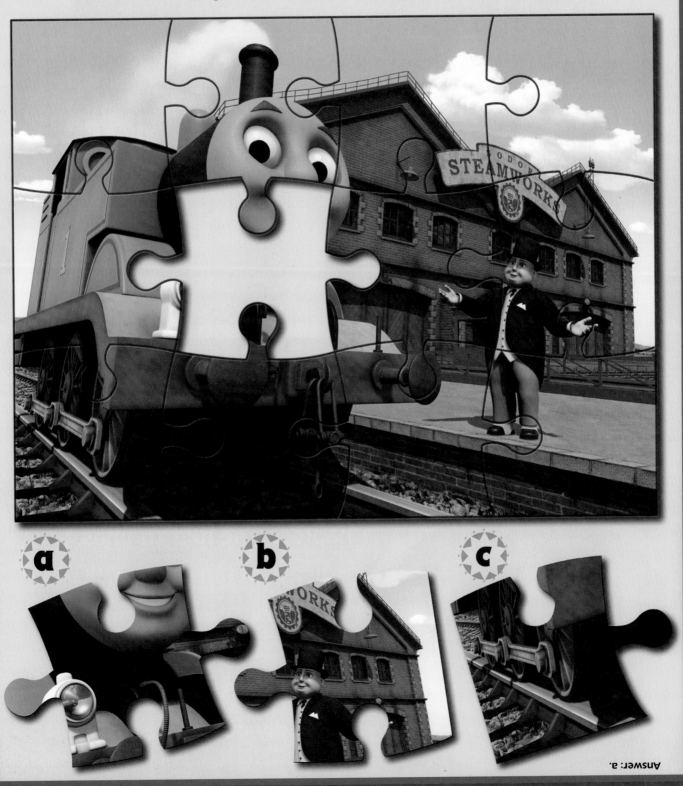

a

b

c

The Lion of Sodor

It was a beautiful day, and Thomas was puffing down to Brendam Docks. He had a very **special** Special to collect! Cranky lowered a wooden crate on to Thomas' flatbed.

"The Mayor is waiting for this at Knapford," he told Thomas.

"It's the Lion of Sodor!"

"I've never carried a **real lion** before!" Thomas smiled, as he puffed proudly out of the Docks.

On his way to Knapford, Thomas passed Henry, who was delivering **sticky treacle**. Thomas asked Henry if he could have some treacle for the lion to eat, and kind Henry agreed. So Henry's Driver poured some treacle into the lion's crate.

"Thank you, Henry!" Thomas called as he puffed away. Next he saw Edward, who happily gave Thomas some of the fresh fish he was carrying for the lion.

"Thank you, Edward!" said Thomas as he started off along the tracks. "I'd better not be late for the Mayor!"

Just outside Knapford, Thomas saw Toby the Tram Engine puffing along his tracks.

He was carrying straw, and both the engines agreed that the lion might like some.

Toby's Driver scattered some straw into the top of the crate, and off Thomas chuffed.

Thomas puffed proudly into Knapford Station. Lots of people and engines had gathered to see the Lion of Sodor.

The workmen carefully opened the crate, and there was a gasp from the crowd.

The Lion of Sodor wasn't a real lion at all! It was a statue, and now it was covered in **treacle**, **fish** and **straw**.

Thomas' cheeks went as red as James!

"I'm sorry," said Thomas. "I thought the lion was real, and wanted to take **extra special** care of it."

"What a mess!" said The Fat Controller. "And the Mayor is due at tea time!"

"I'll get it clean and shiny again in no time, I promise, Sir!" Thomas puffed as The Fat Controller went back to his car.

Then Henry steamed up next to Thomas. "Why don't you take the lion to the wash down?" he said, kindly.

It was a very good idea, so Thomas pumped his pistons and puffed away as quickly as possible.

Soon the sticky mess was washed off and the Lion of Sodor was clean again. But it still wasn't shiny! So Thomas took it to the Steamworks to be polished.

Afterwards, the statue sparkled in the sun. It was ready to go back to Knapford!

Everyone wanted to see the Lion of Sodor, and as Thomas chuffed through the countryside to Knapford, children and passengers **cheered**. When Thomas puffed into Knapford Station, the Mayor had just arrived.

"Well done, Thomas," smiled the Mayor. "This is the finest statue I've ever seen."

And Thomas smiled from funnel to footplate!

Story Quiz

Now you've read about Thomas' adventure with the Lion of Sodor, see if you can answer these questions. **Tick the right answers** for the questions below.

1 Where was Thomas taking the Lion of Sodor?

a Knapford ☐

b Farmer Trotter's farm ☐

c Tidmouth Sheds ☐

2 Who was waiting for the Lion of Sodor at Knapford?

a The Mayor ☐

b Farmer Trotter ☐

c The Thin Controller ☐

3 Who was carrying the treacle?

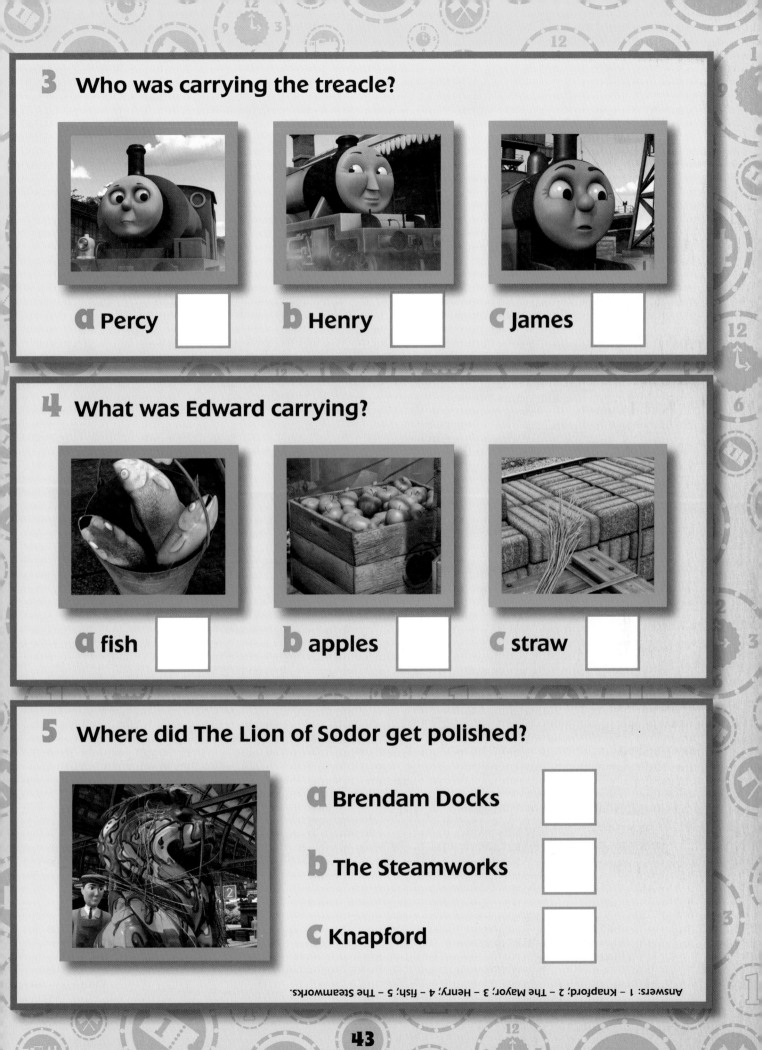

a Percy

b Henry

c James

4 What was Edward carrying?

a fish

b apples

c straw

5 Where did The Lion of Sodor get polished?

a Brendam Docks

b The Steamworks

c Knapford

Answers: 1 – Knapford; 2 – The Mayor; 3 – Henry; 4 – fish; 5 – The Steamworks.

43

Name Game

Do you know the names of all these Sodor engines?

Circle **two** engines on this page whose name begins with **T**.

FREDDIE

★ Colour Bertie ★

Meet Bertie the Bus!
Join the dots to draw him, then colour him in, using the little picture as a guide.

Now trace over the letters to write Bertie's name.

Bertie

Thomas and the Kite

You can help read this story. The little pictures will help you. When you see the pictures of Thomas and his friends, say their names.

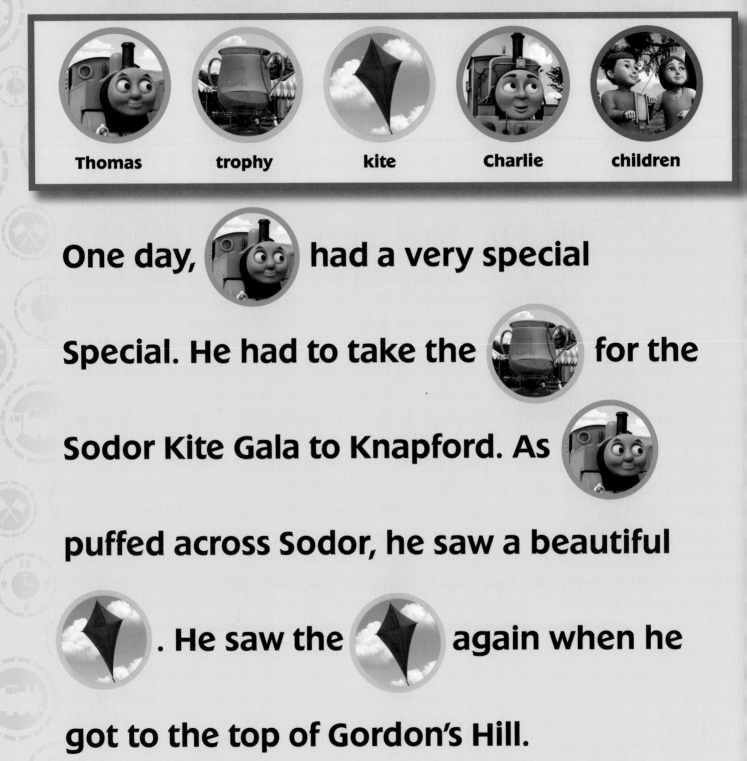

Thomas   **trophy**   **kite**   **Charlie**   **children**

One day, [Thomas] had a very special

Special. He had to take the [trophy] for the

Sodor Kite Gala to Knapford. As [Thomas]

puffed across Sodor, he saw a beautiful

[kite]. He saw the [kite] again when he

got to the top of Gordon's Hill.

It belonged to some .

Suddenly, a strong gust of wind blew

the . It flew up, up and away.

wanted to help get it back.

"Don't be sad,"  said to the .

"I can catch your !"

And off wheeshed.

 chased the along the tracks.

His boiler bubbled and his coal crackled.

But wasn't quite fast enough.

No matter how much he chased and

raced, he couldn't catch the  .

Soon, 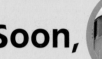 had run out of coal! He was

very worried. He still hadn't delivered the

 or caught the  .

Just then, came chuffing along the

tracks and lent 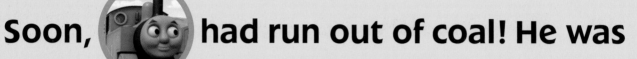 some coal.

The two engines chuffed to Knapford

together and delivered the  .

The  were sad. They hoped

would find their  . They climbed on

board  to look for it together.

Thomas' friends Emily, Edward and

helped too. Working together, they

found the  ! **Hooray!**  was

very happy to have such good friends.

And he was even happier to see the

and their  in the Gala later!

Close-ups

Thomas is helping Kevin at the Steamworks.

These close-ups can all be found in the **big picture**, except one. Tick the boxes as you find them to see which is the **odd one out**.

a

b

c

d

e

f

Answer: e is not in the big picture.

51

Thomas and the Pigs

Thomas loved visiting all the farms on Sodor, but his **favourite** was Farmer Trotter's pig farm. One day, Farmer Trotter had some exciting news.

"One of my pigs is going to have piglets today," he told Thomas. "Could you collect some soft straw for them from Farmer McColl's Farm?"

Thomas was happy to help. He couldn't wait to see the little piglets! He chuffed cheerfully off along the track to Farmer McColl's Farm.

As he whizzed over the rails, Thomas couldn't stop thinking about the piglets and whether they would like anything other than the straw.

As he puffed past the Dairy, he saw Percy, getting ready to deliver milk.

"May I have some milk for Farmer Trotter's piglets?" Thomas asked him.

Percy laughed. "Of course!" he said, as the milk churns were loaded into Thomas' truck. Thomas chuffed on across Sodor, still thinking about the piglets. James gave him some juicy apples for them at the Orchard, and some children helped him gather shiny brown chestnuts in the woods for them too. Soon, everyone on Sodor was excited about the piglets! At last, Thomas chuffed into Farmer McColl's yard.

"Thomas, you are late," Farmer McColl said. He was not very happy, especially when he looked in Thomas' truck.

"Your truck is full," he said. "There's **no room** for the piglets' straw!"

Thomas hadn't thought about that!

"I must puff back to Farmer Trotter's farm right now" he said, pumping his pistons as he chuffed quickly away.

When he arrived back at the pig farm, Farmer Trotter wasn't very happy either.

"Piglets need soft straw," the Farmer told Thomas. "They'll be born very soon!"

Thomas felt very **silly**. He emptied his

truck as fast as he could. He had to pick up that straw! He whooshed and wheeshed through the countryside, past Percy, James and the children. They all wanted to know about the piglets.

"Sorry, I can't stop," Thomas peeped back at them.

He picked up the straw and **rushed** back to Farmer Trotter's farm.

But when Thomas arrived back there, there were no pigs in sight. Thomas was sure he was too late, when a voice came out of the darkness.

"You're **just in time**, Thomas!" It was Farmer Trotter. He opened the shed doors, and there lay the mother pig and her piglets.

They were even sweeter than Thomas had thought, and he was even happier when Farmer Trotter told him he had named one of the piglets ... **Thomas!**

Milk Maze

In the story, Percy was delivering milk. Guide him through the maze to **collect** eight shiny milk churns.

Start

Finish

Memory Test

Look at this picture of Thomas at Farmer McColl's Farm for a minute, then cover it up and answer the questions below.

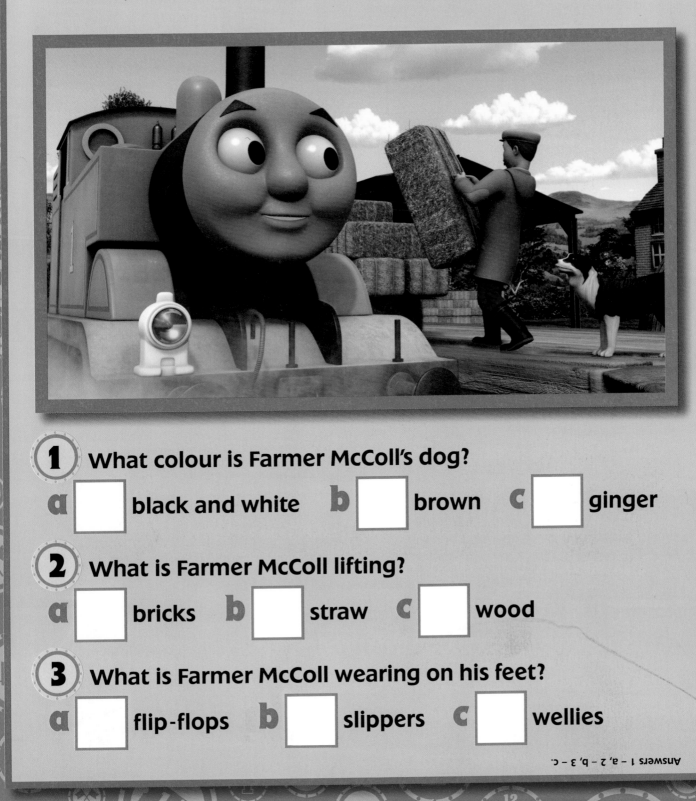

1 What colour is Farmer McColl's dog?

a ☐ black and white   **b** ☐ brown   **c** ☐ ginger

2 What is Farmer McColl lifting?

a ☐ bricks   **b** ☐ straw   **c** ☐ wood

3 What is Farmer McColl wearing on his feet?

a ☐ flip-flops   **b** ☐ slippers   **c** ☐ wellies

Answers 1 – a, 2 – b, 3 – c.

59

Snow Tracks

It was wintertime on the Island of Sodor, and the tracks were covered in **deep snow**. The Fat Controller needed some trucks to be taken to Brendam Docks, so he asked Gordon, one of his strongest engines, to take them.

"Snow is slippery, Gordon," The Fat Controller warned him. "Go **around** hills, not **over** them."

"Yes, Sir," Gordon replied.

After The Fat Controller had left, Gordon was huffing and puffing with pride.

"I will steam **over** every hill I come to!" he boasted. "I'm the strongest and the best!"

With that, Gordon wheeshed out of Tidmouth Sheds, leaving all of the other engines behind. Soon, he was chuffing across Sodor, with his smoke grey against the snowy countryside. He sped on to Gordon's Hill, though the snow was getting **deeper and deeper**. It was very hard work to chuff through the thick snow, but proud Gordon would not admit it.

"Gordon's Hill isn't too steep for me! I shall steam over it!" he tooted, though his wheels were aching already and his boiler felt ready to burst.

Gordon huffed up the steep hill through the thick snow. But instead of being pushed to the side, the snow was piling up in front of him. Soon Gordon was pushing a huge **snowball!** It grew bigger and bigger until it got so heavy that it started to push Gordon back down the hill.

Just then, Thomas puffed up behind Gordon. He was delivering firewood to the Stationmasters so they wouldn't get cold.

"Watch out, Thomas!" cried Gordon, as he rolled back faster and faster.

Thomas raced off into a siding, but it was too late!

Gordon managed to slide out of the way, but the giant snowball **crashed** straight into Thomas and his trucks, knocking them off the rails!

Gordon felt terrible. **"This is a disaster!"** he said, sadly. "I'm so sorry, Thomas. I'll try to push you back on to the rails."

But Gordon was too tired from puffing through all the snow. He wasn't strong enough to get his friend back on the tracks.

"I know what to do! Don't worry, Thomas!" Gordon called, and he steamed off down the rails.

When he returned, he brought Rocky with him, who used his strong crane arm to lift Thomas back on to the rails.

"**Thank you, Rocky!**" Thomas beamed. "Now I must deliver my firewood. The Stationmasters must be very cold by now!"

"I will help you, Thomas," Gordon told him, and together they chuffed off to all the stations on Sodor, and the Docks too. Thomas was very glad to have his friend with him, and Gordon had learnt his lesson – whenever they came to a hill, they puffed **around** it!

Who's Next?

Look at these lines of pictures.

Who should come next in each row?

Say their names out loud.

1

Thomas   James   Thomas   James   Thomas

2

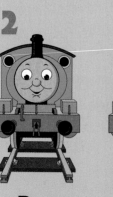    

Percy   Percy   Freddie   Freddie   Percy

3

Toby   Emily   Henry   Toby   Emily

Colour Thomas

Peep! Peep! Thomas is puffing back to Tidmouth Sheds after a hard day's work. Colour him in, then join in singing his special song on the next page.

Use these colours!

blue

red

yellow

brown

black

Sing Along!

They're two, they're four, they're six, they're eight,

Shunting trucks and hauling freight,

Red and green and brown and blue,

They're the Really Useful crew!

All with different roles to play

Round Tidmouth Sheds or far away.

Down the hills and round the bends,

Thomas and his friends.

Thomas he's the cheeky one,
James is vain but lots of fun.
Percy pulls the mail on time,
Gordon thunders down the line.
Emily really knows her stuff,
Henry toots and huffs and puffs.
Edward wants to help and share,
Toby, well let's say – he's square!

See you next year,
Goodbye!